FLOUNDER BYTES

RONALD TRACY

FLOUNDER BYTES

RONALD TRACY

www.flounderbytes.com

ACKNOWLEDGEMENTS

This is dedicated to all of my family and friends who persevered with me during the course of writing and photographing the contents of this book. In my quest to help others learn about flounder fishing I was fortunate because help was there for me whenever I asked... and it came in many forms.

I thank God for my family and friends. For all the blessings he has given me in my life, for creating such a diversity of fish, wildlife and ecosystems that enable me to do what I enjoy; fish, write and share my knowledge with others.

To my girl Sherree, I can't thank you enough for all of your faith, encouragement and help while writing this book. It really means a lot to me.

To my sons Mike, Ron and Greg for all the memorable trips we have shared together and for teaching me to follow my dreams, a heartfelt thank you.

To my good friend and fishing buddy Chuck, with whom I have shared many, many fishing adventures throughout the years, I thank you for your patience and good humor during the course of this endeavor. There will always be a place in my boat for you and hopefully there will be many more fishing adventures in our future.

I owe a very special thank you to my good friend Billy Quinn for the constant supply of hand-tied bucktails and teasers I have used while fishing and photographing for this book.

To my buddy Greg Baker, for putting together my computer system and offering help whenever I need it, even from thousands of miles away. Thank you.

I am grateful to the Captains I have interviewed for sharing some of their knowledge and expertise of flounder fishing and what to look for in good locations and in bait choices.

And I definitely owe my long time friend and saltwater mentor Bill Kephart a very special thank you for all he has taught me throughout the years. Everyone should have the good fortune to have a friend and teacher like Bill.

To my friend Jason for helping with the graphics, computer and film work, thank you.

And to Richie… thanks for being there and helping me see this through.

CONTENTS

Introduction 1

Stack the Odds in Your Favor 3

Choosing the Right Bait to Get Started 7

Choosing the Right Gear 1 1

Let's Go Fishing 1 3

Marking Fish Location 1 7

Why Spinner-Rigs Are So Effective 2 1

Jigs 2 5

Teasers 3 1

Let the Fish Be Your Guide 3 7

Deep-Water Fishing 4 3

Targeting Big Flounder 4 7

What Captains Have To Say 5 1

Ronald Tracy 5 5

Glossary 6 1

INTRODUCTION

A Few Facts about the Summer Flounder

From early May and throughout the summer months one of the most sought after inshore fish species in the North East United States is the summer flounder or fluke. Undoubtedly this fish is a staple of charter, head boats, the rental fleet and private boaters alike during this time period. Bank, jetty and surf fishermen also take their fair share of flatfish as well; and with good reason: "This is one opportunistic fish, it makes for great table fare and it is abundant!"

Each spring these fish migrate into our bays, backwaters and estuaries to spawn and feed. The fish are around throughout most of the summer months before they begin their migration to the wintering grounds offshore during the late summer and early autumn months. During the summer months the fish are easily accessible to anglers all along our coastlines, back-bays and creeks as they are widely dispersed. This is when the inshore action for this species is at its peak.

By design, flounder are primarily bottom feeders and rarely pass up a meal within easy reach. This, along with the ability to bury and blend into the bottom surroundings, makes them excellent ambush predators. As anglers, we will use this knowledge to our advantage, learn how to put it to good use and join in on the action. The techniques in this book consistently work for me and can work for you too.

I have included a few video links that you may find helpful and while you are there I encourage you to subscribe and receive automatic updates on future postings. It's free and you can stay informed. Also the Flounder Bytes e-book version makes for a handy reference guide and fits on your smart phone for when you are out fishing.

Finally, you can unlock the information needed to locate **"high percentage"** areas along with the baits, tackle and techniques that flounder find hard to resist. So let's get started!

STACK THE ODDS IN YOUR FAVOR

Knowing our target species is a bottom dweller helps to eliminate several layers of the water column. This is why most experienced flounder anglers try to stay in contact with the bottom at all times.

And even though they are very strong swimmers it is important to note that while flounder will chase bait, they won't chase it very far. The exceptions are when a fish is very hungry or when they are schooled up and competition for food is high, such as in the early spring before large schools of baitfish become active. The latter becomes evident when you see more than one flounder following your bait on the retrieve. When this happens a slight pause on the retrieve (to let the offering slowly fall through the strike zone) is usually all it takes to get a fish to slam your offering.

Flounder are bottom dwellers by design; therefore, it is important to fish your baits on - or close to - the bottom in order to stay in their strike or feeding zone. Another interesting fact is: flounder are very adept at burying and blending into the bottom surroundings and patiently waiting for prey to come along. This is why drift fishing works so well! This is the predatory nature of the flounder. They are also a very opportunistic fish and rarely pass up a meal within easy reach.

Getting Started

In late April and early May, when flounder start moving into the bays and backwater areas, there are not a whole lot of baitfish moving around. Crabs are coming out of hibernation, bugs are almost non-existent and the water temperature is in the low to mid 50's. For the warm water species we are after, the bay is just starting to come back to life.

So, what bait do we use and why?

Because the primary food source is not as active, as when the water temperature is higher, flounder simply cannot afford to be that partial to any particular bait in general. Cut baits, such as mackerel, clam and squid strips are all effective. Small jigs, tipped with a strip of squid and/or minnow combination is a deadly tactic during the early season and will usually trigger an aggressive bite when nothing else works.

Locating Your Quarry

The best places to start in locating a school of hungry fish is a bait and tackle shop or marina in the area that you are going to be fishing. They can point you in the right direction with locations to try first. They have a local knowledge of the water and know what has worked in the past, from rigs and baits, to techniques and tips. However, don't expect exact G.P.S. (Global Positioning System) coordinates. More than likely you will get a general area to help you get started. Finding the fish and getting them to bite is entirely up to you.

Don't be afraid to ask questions!!!

Arm yourself with information. The more information you have the better equipped you will be to eliminate non-productive areas, increase your valuable fishing time and your chances of a successful outing.

There just may be a particular jig, rig, or color combination that the fish have been clobbering that you may not have in your tackle arsenal. If so, ask if they carry it and buy some along with your bait. It is far better to be prepared.

Once it is known that you are willing to plunk down a few hard earned dollars, they will want you to come back as a repeat customer. Remember, your success is important to their success and usually a more in depth answer will follow. The better the information, the better your chances of getting on fish fast. And the faster you find the fish, the faster you can get down to the business of catching them.

Tidal changes have an effect on the feeding habits of fish and flounder are no exception. Sometimes the incoming tide will see the most feeding activity; sometimes the outgoing tide will be the key, and some days the fish just seem to bite regardless of the tides. Most bait and tackle shops have free tide charts for their area. Be sure and pick one up. Now if you have access to the web you can go online and look up the information before you leave home at: **http://WWW.NWS.NOAA.GOV**.

Next… "Flounder baits that are proven winners!"

CHOOSING THE RIGHT BAIT
TO GET STARTED

Even though the summer flounder is a predator it is also an opportunistic fish, feeding on whatever scraps are filtering down through the water column. Anglers have long known about the big stripers folloswing the ravaging schools of bluefish around and feeding on the remnants of hapless baitfish filtering down through the water column as the blues slash their way through the schools of bunker. The bass grow fat and happy eating scraps of food with very little effort expended on their part. Flounder are no different when the opportunity arises. This is one reason cut baits work so well; it is a natural occurrence within the food chain. Fish are accustomed to seeing chunks of bait filter down through the water. Another reason cut baits work really well is that filleting and cutting the bait into strips disperses the oils and scent into the water attracting the fish to the bait, much like a chum pot. Any good fishing book, article or video will tell you that much.

A frequently asked question is: **"What fish makes the best-cut bait for flounder?"**

It depends on the time of the season and the bait that is available. Springtime in the Northeast means herring and mackerel. Later on into the summer, when the herring and mackerel move on, it can be almost any fish you catch or purchase from the bait shop. Sea robin, flounder belly, and shark belly work well. Just be sure to

7

check the fish & game laws about size limits and any restrictions on the fish you would like to use as bait. Flounder are cannibals. They do eat smaller flounder and flounder-belly; however, anglers must obey the size limits and restrictions imposed by law. That means if you wish to use flounder belly as bait, the flounder you use must make the minimum size limit by law and the laws vary from State to State. Also, some states do not allow the filleting of fish at sea, unless you are on a registered charter boat so be safe and check the regulations where you intend to fish.

When you take into consideration the vast and varied diet of the flounder, its predatory nature; its opportunistic (almost scavenger-like tendencies) combined with the profile of an easy to swallow and appealing bait, you have a win – win situation. That is especially good for large flounder. Now let's move on to some more commonly used baits that make up a large portion of the flounder's diet... minnows.

http://youtu.be/7EXb5saMtag

The stout, yet slender profile of the common minnow is extremely appealing to the flounder and at times they will gorge themselves almost exclusively on minnows. Minnows are the bait of choice of many serious flounder anglers... that says a lot about the appeal this bait has on our target species.

When fishing for flounder, I never leave the dock without them and there is a good reason for this...flounder key in on minnows!

Whenever I am trying to locate an actively feeding school of flounder one of the first baits I use is a minnow. It may be used on a jig, or maybe on a spinner-rig, or even on a plain hook all by itself. But, one thing I am sure of... if there is a flounder in the area; it's going to hit the minnow!

Minnows can be fished alone, on a spinner-rig, or fished on a jig to add scent and appeal. They often work when other baits go untouched. This is one offering you do not want to be without. Let's move along to an awesome flounder bait and one of my favorites.

Spearing

The spearing is one of the most productive baitfish an angler can use and when they show up in the net, I will use them almost exclusively. This baitfish is that good... and flounder love them! However, they are a fragile fish and don't keep long in a bait well, or on a hook. They don't freeze well either. They turn to mush when they thaw out, so this bait is best caught and used fresh. You can fish them the same as you do minnows, only use a barrel swivel on your line or you will end up with a tangled mess, as this bait tends to curl once it expires. But that curl is a big part of the appeal as it spirals along near the bottom in an erratic motion that drives flounder wild.

Here is another-good bait for flounder that is often overlooked:

Grass Shrimp

The grass shrimp is incredible bait for flounder. The scent these little guys give off is like ringing the dinner bell to fish... almost magical! They are like flounder magnets. They have an amazing draw on the fish. Anglers fishing for weakfish (sea trout) often anchor and toss out handfuls to attract the fish to the boat through the currents. It has the same affect on flounder. I like to use them as an added attractant while jig fishing and also on my spinner-rigs simply because they really attract the fish... and I get some downright mean strikes. When a flounder goes after a grass shrimp it eats it with a reckless abandon. It does not mouth it like a minnow; instead... it clobbers the bait and usually winds up hooking itself. Now that's my kind of fishing. There is "no" mistake about the bite or that you have a fish on the end of your line!

Up next... the basic gear you will need to get started!

CHOOSING THE RIGHT GEAR

Even though the summer flounder is a saltwater fish, it is not a huge fish by any standard. Eight and ten-pound fish are caught every season and some push the fourteen-pound range or larger. Choosing the right gear is dependent upon the average water depth, water current and wind conditions in the area you intend to fish. Swift currents and deep water require more weight or heavy jigs to remain in contact with the bottom. You will also need a rod with enough backbone to handle the additional weight and to muscle fish up from the depths. Here is what to look for in equipment.

Medium to medium/heavy action tackle 6-7 foot rod lengths is more than enough to handle even the largest flounder you may encounter while adding plenty of sport to your fishing experience. Your reel choice should match the rod action, have a smooth drag system and balance the rod/reel combination in your hand. Both conventional and spinning gear work well for flounder fishing and which gear you use is a matter of personal preference.

Line choice. Braided line in 30lb. test has the same diameter of 8lb. test monofilament and is a good all around choice for bottom fishing. Many flounder, especially big flounder, tend to suck bait in and bury into the bottom extremely quick. The big fish stick to the bottom like glue and can be tough to break loose. It takes consistent rod pressure and a strong line to budge these doormats off of the bottom. Once free of the bottom you need to keep the fish swimming up to the boat and in the water until you can bring them to the net. A word of advice: do not allow a large flounder to thrash around on top of the water. The thrashing action along with the weight of the fish can tear the hook out and your dinner will swim away.

Sinkers. An assortment of sinkers ranging from ½ up to 4-ounces in weight will cover most bay and backwater fishing situations. My preference is bait-walking sinkers. The side-to-side walking motion imparts an erratic action to the bait as it is pulled or drifted along the bottom.

Jigs. An assortment of lead-head jigs in ¼ to 3-ounces in various colors and patterns will help you to maintain bottom contact and high visibility in the water. Popular and productive bucktail jig colors are red & white, orange, chartreuse, green, and blue & white in a mackerel pattern. I always have at least one rod rigged with a jig and in the water at all times. The reason is simple. Big flounder love jigs and I love to catch big flounder!

Hooks and Flounder rigs. A basic flounder rig consists of a three-foot leader of monofilament line with a loop on one end, one or two spinner blades, some colored beads, a clevis (to attach the blades) and a hook tied onto the other end. The hook may be plain or dressed with colored hair, or a small plastic tube on the shank of the hook. They come fully assembled and ready to fish right out of the package.

The tackle box. Get a tackle box that can handle all of your terminal tackle, like hooks, sinkers, jigs, lures, etc. A good tackle box will help you stay organized and give fast access to your gear.

Last but not least is the net. This is one item you don't want to skimp on... it gets the fish in the boat. Get a wide-mouth, long-handled net and you are ready for action!

LET'S GO FISHING

All ready to go. The boat is loaded with bait, lunch, tackle and beverages. All of the rods have been rigged back at the house to save valuable time while cruising to the first potential hotspot in search of our quarry.

Locating the fish. Upon arriving we need to locate the fish. Hungry fish... active fish. Fish that are going to climb all over our baits and try to pull the rods out of the boat! The easiest and most productive method to do this is drift fishing.

Drift fishing. Drift fishing is simplicity itself. Once you pull up to a location and turn off the engine, the wind and wave currents take over and move your boat around the bay quietly drifting your baits over the waiting fish.

On the initial drift, try as many different offerings as you can get in the water. For example: On one rod I would use a 1-ounce jig, tipped with a minnow directly on the bottom; I would attach a fluke rig, tipped with a strip of squid and a minnow to a barrel swivel 18-24 inches above this and lower this combination to the bottom. On another rod I would attach a sinker directly to the end of the line; 12-inches above this I would attach a 24-inch leader to a barrel swivel, tie on a 3/0 hook and a chunk of cut bait and lower this combination to the bottom. On another rod I may attach a slip-sinker up the line with a barrel swivel for a stop, and a 36-inch leader with a thin wire hook baited with grass shrimp. One of these offerings is bound to work as flounder love these baits!

The objective. The object is to entice the fish with as many baits and combinations as possible and see just which combination is producing the best results. Then it is simply a matter of changing setups on the other rods to duplicate your success.

How long and how far the initial drift should be all depends on the area you are fishing. If you are fishing the vast expanse of a wide-open bay you may want to continue drifting until you actually start catching flounder. Generally, where there is one there are more and they are there for a reason.

If you plan to fish backwater creeks, narrow inlets, or cuts in between islands, your drift will be limited by natural barriers and boat traffic during fishing season. Be aware of your surroundings and practice safe boating procedures at all times. Backwater creek fishing can be extremely productive during the dog days of summer. Many flounder – including some real doormats – are found in the backwater areas by savvy anglers looking to get away from the congestion of boaters on the bay. The points, drop-offs and feeding flats that normally hold fish are easy and quick to find... where the fish are lying will depend upon the tide phase itself.

Tide Tactics

When flounder season is in full swing, chances are they are favoring one tide or another for feeding. That is when most of the anglers are catching fish. This is how tackle shops and marinas get the information that is passed on to other anglers. However, the fish don't disappear just because the tide changes. They are still there and they can still be caught if you are willing to put in the effort. And a little effort can make a big difference in catching fish.

During periods of high, low or ebb tides the fish can still be caught.

14

Flounder like a bait that moves. Baitfish swim, crabs and shrimp scamper and swim, and when wounded, dying or disoriented they move sporadically while drifting downward with the current. The natural instinct of predators is to weed out the sick or injured... drift fishing simulates this natural action with very little effort... the predators (flounder) do the rest.

Sometimes the wind and tide cooperate offering a very decent drift for fishing. Other times the boat drifts "too" fast or "out of control" over the fish resulting in very few (if any) bites at all. In this instance let's explore our options.

Anchor in deep water and drop the baits directly to the bottom... occasionally changing locations until finding the fish. Anchor over a drop-off cast and slowly retrieve the baits back to the boat, covering all the area around the boat before changing locations. Slow troll the area with either the outboard engaged at idle speed or better yet, by using an electric trolling motor.

My preference is the electric trolling motor for a variety of reasons.

Electric trolling motors are quiet, powerful and have variable speed settings.

Boat speed and positioning can be controlled easily. Multiple rods, baits and lures can be used simultaneously. You can troll shallow areas or backwater creeks without spooking the fish with the noise from the outboard motor. Productive areas can be covered with consistency. They are environmentally friendly and very economical to operate.

If you already have a trolling motor use it, if not, consider getting one. They are inexpensive and well worth the investment. It just may help you catch that flounder of a lifetime.

Fishing tip: start with small baits first to locate actively feeding fish and remember... fresh bait works the best!

MARKING FISH LOCATION

An often-overlooked item in our fishing arsenal is the marker buoy and its use. A marker buoy is a floating device with a weight attached to a line or rope. It is used to mark underwater structure, drop-offs, channels, submerged points and fish location. Think of it as a simple form of Global Positioning System without all the bells and whistles.

The use of marker buoys has been around for a long time. Fresh water bass anglers use them all the time, so why not use them for flounder fishing. Only we will use the marker buoy to target the flounders' actual location and afterwards as a visual reference aid. Here is how to do it using the information we have gathered so far.

Upon reaching the target area: We will start by determining the direction and speed the boat is going to drift. This will be dictated by the wind, the tide phase and the actual weight of your boat. Stop the boat, shift the engine into neutral or shut it off completely and allow the boat to drift freely. This will determine the speed and direction of your drift. On the downward side of your drift, drop a baited set-up into the water and allow the offering to fall freely to the bottom. Line will stop paying off the reel when the weight hits the bottom. Allow out approximately twice as much line as the water depth. You should be able to feel the weight dragging across the bottom through the fishing rod. This will be indicated by a pulsing or throbbing action at the rod tip. This action will let you know if your bait is hugging the bottom and near the strike zone of the flounder. You can adjust the weight accordingly to stay in contact with the bottom.

Now you can adjust the weight on all your rigs and send them to the bottom. At this point it is important to place a variety of offerings into the strike zone to determine what (if any) preference the fish have. Remember… the more lines you have in the water the more chances you have of hooking up. At this point you are ready to start catching fish and gather more information, only this time from the fish themselves.

Let's assume that flounder season is in full swing.

It's mid-June; the fish are spread throughout the bays, backwaters and inlets. The fish are everywhere and cooperative. One of the rods in the boat goes down… you've got a fish on the line. Here is where the marker buoy comes into play. It should be kept as handy as the net and ready for deployment at all times. When the fish is hooked is when the marker buoy should be tossed over the side of the boat. This is how to mark the actual location of the fish.

Remember, where there is one there are more and if you wait until after landing the fish in the boat, chances are you will have drifted or trolled past the actual location of actively feeding fish. The sooner you drop the buoy the better your chances of finding the fish and hooking up again. How long and far you should drift is entirely up to you and the surroundings. However, unless you are catching fish, I would not drift out of sight of the marker buoy. Remember, this is a visual reference of where active fish are located. If your boat is equipped with a global positioning system (GPS) make a note of the grid coordinates. By returning to the coordinates you return to the fish.

If you drift one hundred yards and do not catch another fish, reel in the lines, start the engine and run back past the marker buoy and start another drift. Try drifting or slow trolling the area all around the marker buoy increasing the distance with every pass. Make a mental note of where any fish are caught in relation to the marker buoy and what bait (or baits) the fish hit on. By doing this you will be able to tell if the fish are on the move or are feeding in the area and you just may find one or two setups are catching the majority of the fish. Duplicate these setups on other rods to increase your hookup rate.

Fishing Productive Areas

When you have located an actively feeding school of flounder and have the location marked with a buoy (or GPS coordinates) you have a few options as to your actual fishing methods and bait presentations. If drift fishing continues to yield fish (in a relatively confined area) inside of your targeted and marked location, the most productive method may be to anchor up and cast stationary baits into the feeding zone letting the flounder come to you. This method saves a lot of wasted time in needless boat movement during the drift and running back to your location. By soaking the baits in the same location you create a scent trail that draws the fish in looking for the food source, much like a chum pot does.

Try slow trolling. Keep in mind that winds, currents and tides change throughout the day and fish tend to move following the bait. Be prepared to change with the conditions and try other methods like fan casting the area all around the boat or try slow trolling in ever widening circles around the marker buoy and against the original drift pattern. The presentation of baits in this manner is often more than flounder can stand and generally an aggressive strike will follow.

The instinctive strike. A key to triggering an instinctive strike from this predator is to vary the trolling speed and boat direction. This will make the baits to appear disoriented and an easy target for the flounder. If you are using flounder rigs with attached spinner blades (and you should be) stop the trolling motor intermittently or kick the engine out of gear. This will cause the spinner blades to stop spinning and flutter down towards the bottom acting as a wounded or dying baitfish. Remember... It is a natural instinct for predators to weed out the injured, disorientated or weak.

If there is a fish in the area this erratic action will not go unnoticed. This method is particularly effective when fish are in a negative feeding mode and works awesome on big flounder.

Fishing tip: Do not cast, drift or retrieve a fishing line over the line attached to the marker buoy. Fishing hooks are sharp for a reason and they can become attached to the buoy line.

WHY SPINNER-RIGS ARE SO EFFECTIVE

T he blades of a spinner-rig are there to add flash and vibration. This is meant to get the attention of the fish. Like most fish, flounder have what is called a lateral line. It is a pencil-thin line running down the back of the flounder and is used to detect vibrations in the water. In dark or murky water fish use this lateral line to key in on their prey. When swimming, baitfish-emit vibrations in the water that other fish sense through their lateral lines. A baitfish that swims in an erratic motion is cause for any predators in the area to investigate. This is a fact of nature.

Spinner blades spin. This causes vibrations in the water. The flash of the spinner blades is a visual attractant. When the blades stop spinning and start to flutter towards the bottom this is an erratic motion. To a predator that senses this action through the lateral line. This is cause for investigation because this bait is feeling and acting injured. When the predator sees the blades fluttering downwards it is viewed as injured or dying and natural instincts take over to eliminate this individual as quickly as possible.

It is important to keep the blades clear of any vegetation so that they spin freely to attract the fish. Flounder may swim and hide around the various vegetation in the bays, estuaries and oceans, but they do not eat it; instead they eat the shrimp, crabs and assorted baitfish that are attracted to the grasses for food and cover. To work effectively the spinner-rig must ride over the top or alongside the seaweed and grasses. If fishing open water you may have to contend with seaweed, particularly on an incoming tide. Adjust the spinner-rig to ride 2-to-3 feet off of the bottom. Make sure you have at least 18-to-36 inches of leader so the rig can ride over top of the seaweed yet drift towards the bottom occasionally. The flounder will come up and out of the seaweed to get the bait.

When fishing sod-banks and marsh-grass shorelines drift the spinner-rig parallel to the banks, just off the bottom and as close to the banks as you can get. Flounder lay in ambush on the outer fringes of the grass-line waiting for something to venture out. You can also work the area over thoroughly by anchoring and fan casting to the shoreline. Anchor the boat in deeper water and within casting distance of where you feel the fish may be holding. Cast to a target area and let the rig settle to the bottom before retrieving. Keep the weight in constant contact with the bottom while slowly sweeping the rod backwards... enough to move the bait 2-3 feet. Move the rod forward reeling in the slack line and repeat the process back to the boat. The spinner-rig will fall and flutter while reeling in the slack line acting as a wounded or dying baitfish.

Note use of the spinner-rig in this method may require multiple casts to the same target area to get a response from any fish that may be in the area, especially if fishing during an ebb (or slack) tide and here is why:

On the initial cast and retrieve the vibration transmitted by the spinner blades will get the attention of any predator in the area. The fish know something is happening and in what general direction but it may not be in their sight or strike range. 3-4 casts to the same target area will either bring the fish in (due to the activity) or eliminate that offering. Try a few casts with a jig – hopping it back to the boat or try soaking a minnow (or grass shrimp) on a bait-hook and leader before eliminating the area altogether.

Fishing stationary baits in this manner is particularly effective after attracting the fish to your location with the spinner-rig, followed by the jig. When using this method I allot a 5-minute time period when soaking bait before moving on to locate more aggressive fish.

Now let's move on to one of my favorite lures that I absolutely love to use in fresh and saltwater... the jig.

Fine examples of hand tied jigs.

JIGS

One lure that has a broad range of appeal to fish it is the lead-head jig. The jig catches fish in fresh and saltwater and will often produce results when other lures and baits go untouched. Jigs come in a variety of sizes, colors and weights. The old standby is called the bucktail jig. It consists of an upturned hook with a lead ball, melted and cast around the shank of the hook. The body of the jig was tied deer hair, usually made from the tail hairs of deer after a successful hunt. The jigs were painted white while the white hair was tied in place with red thread... a popular color combination that still works today, red and white.

Today's jigs are made with synthetic, rubber or silicone skirts and come in a dazzling array of colors and sizes. They come in flipping, pitching and casting models. Some have spinner blades attached, some have built in rattle chambers, and some are designed to sink extremely slow or extremely fast; they are designed to get the attention of the fish through sight, sound and vibration. And even though these jig models were developed for the more glamorous freshwater species like the largemouth bass and walleye they still have a place in our flounder arsenal because they work.

Please bear in mind that some of these jigs are designed for freshwater use and the corrosive nature of saltwater limits their lifespan substantially. On the upside, jigs are relatively inexpensive. To me, if it helps put flounder in the boat it's well worth the tradeoff.

The nice thing about jigs… they are easy to use and fish love them. The problem is that all kinds of fish love them. It is not uncommon to catch weakfish, bluefish, stripers or sea bass on jigs. These fish inhabit the different water columns on the way down to where the flounder live. And yes… while fishing on the bottom you are going to catch your share of skates and rays also. Jigs are the fish catching machines in your arsenal.

Jigging Methods

Jigs have no action of their own. If you cast one out and it falls to the bottom it's just going to lie there and do nothing. It has no appeal to the fish. It might as well be a rock on the bottom - fish don't eat them either. The angler must bring this bait to life… give it some action - make it stand out and get noticed by the fish, and…

"Make that fish want to instinctively eat the jig."

That's how it works if you want to consistently catch fish using jigs. To better understand the attraction that jigs have on fish we need to explore the method of imparting action into the jig.

The basic jig

It's a fact that flounder love jigs and really big flounder find them hard to pass up. That's why I always have at least one jig in the water at all times. I love to catch big flounder and the basic jig is the ideal tool for the job.

You can drift fish jigs alone or in combination with the spinner-rig. If used together the spinner-rig becomes a teaser for the fish and doubles your efforts using one fishing rod.

Teaser-rigs are an extremely effective method of fishing and a lot of the fish caught will be caught on the teaser. The jig is an added attractant and replaces the weight normally used to stay in contact with the bottom.

All kinds of fish love jigs. Above, flounder on a jig and spinner rig, below a fall striper.

Action and appeal equals success

You can make the jig more appealing to the fish with the addition of fresh bait on the hook. The more common baits are the jig and minnow, a small strip of squid as a trailer or one of my favorites grass shrimp. Flounder love grass shrimp. By adding bait you add scent and bulk to the jig – a large meal for the fish. A combination of two baits that flounder love… Can it get any better than this? You bet. Now we give the jig some action and bring it to life.

At this point it is possible to toss the jig over the side and drag it behind the boat and it will catch some fish. However, we want to bring attention to the jig, make it stand out and get noticed by any predators in the area and try for

the instinctive bite. It doesn't take much. With just a little rod action your bait will come to life and get noticed as a struggling and disoriented morsel bringing out the natural instincts in the flounder.

Start by baiting up and casting out the jig, letting it fall to the bottom. Once in contact with the bottom hold the rod at the 10 o'clock position and slowly sweep the rod to the 12 o'clock position. Drop the rod back to the 10 o'clock position while reeling in the slack line as you go along. If you are drift fishing or trolling you will only need to raise and lower the fishing rod. The movement of the boat will take up the slack line automatically. Try and keep the slack line as taut as possible when lowering the rod tip. You want to stay in contact with the jig at all times. Flounder, like most fish, tend to strike the bait while it is falling. Once the jig hits the bottom and the line is taut, jiggle or shake the rod slightly (for a few seconds) while keeping the jig on the bottom. This will impart a sporadic struggling action to the bait while kicking up tufts of sand, silt or bottom debris giving your bait that lifelike appearance. This action is more than flounder can stand and quite often triggers some vicious strikes. Click on the following link and watch a prime example of this method in "The 1 Minute Flounder."

Remember, flounder are bottom feeders and ambush predators. They rely more on stealth and camouflage, however, they can swim very fast.

The upward sweep of the rod imparts a fleeing action to the jig; the downward falling motion means an injured victim, while the skittering action on the bottom represents a natural struggle. Repeating this action is the key to this method of jig fishing.

This bears repeating, while flounder will chase bait, they won't chase it very far. However, they will follow a potential meal and watch its actions – sometimes for quite a distance -- waiting for the opportune moment to strike. I have had the rare good fortune to actually witness firsthand, the stalking, camouflage ability and predatory nature of these stealthy fish in action on more then one occasion. It is quite impressive and there will be more about this later.

Coming up next is without a doubt one of the most productive and exciting flounder baits I have ever encountered in forty-years of fishing. It's the teaser… and does this baby catch fish!

TEASERS

The use of teasers to help catch fish has been around for a long, long time. Striper fishermen have been using this technique successfully for many years. Savvy freshwater anglers utilize this technique to attract more bites from inactive fish and now, we will add this method to our arsenal to help catch more flounder. Yes... catch more flounder!

The addition of a teaser is an extremely powerful way of attracting flounder to your main offering. Due to its lightweight it tends to dart and dance on the slightest of currents occasionally drifting downward mimicking an injured baitfish. Yes, water currents really bring this little gem to life!

These natural actions make it stand out and draw attention to itself with very little effort imparted by the angler. In turn, the erratic movements are noticed by any predators in the area and are cause for investigation. Quite often the teaser is eaten long before the main offering is even noticed and can account for substantially more fish being brought to the net. As a tool, the teaser is this effective. Now, let's examine the composition of a highly effective teaser that we want to have in our flounder arsenal.

https://www.youtube.com/watch?v=17RTMn1_pVY

Since flounder are primarily a bottom feeding saltwater fish, the hardware of our teaser should consist of a strong high-quality saltwater hook. Keep in mind that the teaser has to travel through the water column on its way to the bottom and a well-designed teaser does appeal to a wide variety of fish species within this water column. With the teeth most saltwater fish have a strong hook is a prerequisite. The body should be slim and tied with hair or synthetic fibers directly to the shank of the hook. Large eyes are a plus (adding appeal), as our teaser should resemble a baitfish. And I like a two-tone color to add realism but it's not critical to catching fish.

Teasers are most effective when used in combination with other baits or lures... such as jigs. They can be fished alone and will catch fish. However, their effectiveness is increased tremendously when it appears that they are being chased by (or following) the lure or jig. This appeals to both the predatory and opportunistic nature of flounder. The reason is simple, small baitfish is a staple of the flounders diet (which is why we want our teaser to resemble a baitfish) and they are also known to eat jigs. This is why the jig and teaser combination works so well together. Both baits appeal to the fish. Is this cool or what!

The teaser is a lure that can be fished effectively in many ways. Its profile and characteristics make it very appealing to all kinds of fish. This lure is so lifelike in the water you'd swear it is alive. It's that good. This is the kind of tool we want and look to include in our arsenal for flounder.

Now that we know what a teaser is, what to look for in a teaser, what makes them so effective and why we should use them, let's move on to how we rig them to catch the fish we are after... flounder!

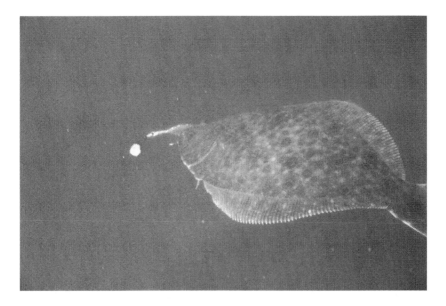

Teasers often account for a large percentage of the fish caught.

The teaser lends itself to fly-fishing due to its lightweight. However, unless the flounder are feeding in the shallows (as they often do) it may be difficult getting the teaser down into their strike zone without some form of weight or weighted fly line. But, this does not rule out fly-fishing for these fish. I have caught flounder on a fly rod and it is exhilarating to say the least. However, I had my suspicions that a mutiny was forming amongst the crew as the reel kept screaming and it taking so long to get the fish into the boat. My suspicions were confirmed when I was threatened with being thrown overboard with the broken rod stuffed into a normally concealed part of my anatomy. If you are going to fish with a fly rod, you may want to fish with others who appreciate this form of fishing. At least... clear it with the crew!

Another productive method (and one that gets the bait down to the fish) is with the use of a slip sinker. Slide the sinker onto the line and attach a barrel swivel to the end of the line. The sinker should slide freely up and down the line with the swivel acting as a stop for the sinker. Attach a two-foot leader to the swivel and tie the teaser to the end of the leader. Lower this to the bottom and hang onto the rod. If you want to use bait, I suggest a live minnow or shrimp. The buoyancy of these baits will still allow the teaser to remain effective.

Now, let's move on to the jig and teaser combination.

There are two main ways that I fish the jig and teaser combination. One is to have the teaser following the jig from above and behind; the other way is to have the jig chasing the teaser.

To tie the above and behind rig: first attach a three-way swivel to the end of the fishing line. Tie a jig onto a two-foot leader and attach it to the bottom of the three-way swivel. Tie a teaser onto a two-foot leader and attach it to the side eyelet of the swivel. When placed into the water, the teaser will drift up and behind the jig. When fishing this rig, most of the fish will be caught on the teaser. It is a good setup to locate the fish.

To tie the chasing rig: attach a three-way swivel to the end of the fishing line. Tie a jig onto a three-foot leader and attach it to the bottom of the swivel. Tie the teaser onto an eighteen-inch leader and attach it to the side eyelet of the swivel. When lowered into the water, the jig will always be behind the teaser moving slower due to its weight. The teaser is used to attract the fish to the jig.

Another way of fishing our teaser is to suspend it under a float. This method works particularly well when fishing the shallow water flats and sand bars that flounder like to frequent when searching for a food source such as minnows, worms and small crustaceans. Float fishing for flounder is very popular in the southern portion of our country. Here's how you rig up for this style of fishing.

Tie the teaser directly to the end of your fishing line and pinch on a split shot (or two) about eighteen-inches above the teaser. Clip the float onto your line anywhere from three to six-feet above the teaser. Cast out, letting the wind and tide move the teaser around near the bottom.

If you are not sure of the water depth, a bobber stop and a slip float can be used (and adjusted) to get your bait down to the fish without snagging on the bottom. You may have to experiment a little to achieve the proper depth of your offering. The split shots are there to help get the teaser down and keep it in the strike zone. The float is to help keep it off the bottom and control the depth of the lure. This set up also works well with live bait.

There is one more way to help maximize the action a teaser can generate while in the water and that is to attach the teaser onto the line with a loop knot. This will allow the teaser to dart and dance on the slightest of currents and help give it that lifelike appearance we are trying to achieve. These actions are similar to the actual movements of a baitfish while swimming and feeding. All this action with very little effort... is this a great little lure or what?

As you can see, this little gem of a lure can be fished successfully in many ways and this is why we want the teaser in our flounder arsenal.

A selection of jigs and teasers in assorted weights, colors and sizes can help you be prepared for various fishing situations.

LET THE FISH BE YOUR GUIDE

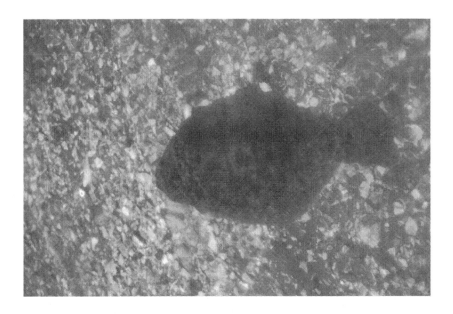

My friends and I were fishing the channels and creeks around some small islands in an area known as Great Bay out of Tuckerton, New Jersey. It was early July; bright and sunny with an incoming tide that brought gin clear water filtering into the bay. Up to that point we had very little success. Fishing reports at the marina had the flounder stacked up everywhere in the bay. So with the tide rolling in and a favorable breeze we decided to drift fish the shallow flats in the hopes that our luck would change.

With our lines over the side of the boat we drifted, and drifted, and drifted until we noticed something odd in the water behind our boat. It was my bait and sinker dragging behind. Through the clear water we could see the subtle changes in the bottom contour and how my bait rig was acting. It wasn't much of a rig, just a minnow on a hook with a sinker to hug the bottom. We watched the tufts of sand rise up as my sinker plodded along while the boat gently rocked back and forth to the rhythm of the wind and the waves. Each rocking motion caused the tufts of sand to appear from my sinker and each time the sinker stopped my minnow would start to drift downward occasionally trying to swim upwards with short spurts of energy, but always drifting back downward. It was during a pause in the rocking that we noticed a small cloud of sand kick up a few feet behind my bait, which was fluttering downwards. To our surprise a flounder slowly swam up to within inches of my sinker and settled down into the sand. We could see its eyes were fixed on the tiring minnow. As the boat drifted onward the flounder stayed in the sand, still watching the minnow with a fixed gaze. The flounder did not move again until the minnow started drifting downwards. Each time the flounder would swim and settle within inches of the sinker. We were fascinated and frustrated as we watched this event unfold. Obviously the fish was interested in the bait, but why? The flounder would not let the minnow travel more than five-feet before swimming after it and settle into the sand.

Even though the water was no more then three-feet deep the minnow never had a chance to make it to the bottom or (as we now know) the acceptable strike zone for the flounder. As long as the boat kept moving and pulling the bait away the flounder would follow, so we decided that the next time the flounder got close to the bait I would open the bail on my reel, free spool the line and let the bait stay in one place long enough to sink to the bottom. If that didn't work we were going to move and find a less irritating fish that we couldn't see. Fortunately the boat hadn't drifted five-feet when we witnessed the explosive strike from that determined fish and we learned some valuable lessons about nature and fishing in the process.

Watching that flounder follow the bait for one hundred yards or better haunted my every waking moments and dreams for an entire week. A lot of thinking, planning and ideas came out of that experience. From the actions of the bait to the reactions from the flounder I knew there had to be quicker and more effective methods to get them to bite.

The Second Encounter

The thrill of sight fishing for flounder on the flats was new and exciting. Armed with the knowledge from our first sight fishing experience including some new insights about the predatory nature of the flounder we headed back to the flats behind the islands determined to try some new methods. We arrived at the top of high tide only to find some of the murkiest water we have ever encountered in forty-years of fishing. Sight fishing was definitely not an option!

Armed with various jigs and flounder rigs we were ready to go fishing and put our newfound knowledge to the test. The jigs would definitely fall into the acceptable strike zone of the flounder and hug the bottom while the spinner-rigs would act as teasers. Each rod would have a different set up until we could determine what was working and why. It felt more like a science class than a day of fishing and our anticipation was extremely high, as the fish would grade our presentation.

With barely a hint of breeze and the tide starting to ebb we could expect no action to be imparted from boat movement. Slow trolling with the outboard produced the occasional bluefish but no hookups with the flounder we were after and the summer fleet of boats seemed to be miles away in the distance so we could not exchange fishing information with the other anglers. We really wanted to fish the flats but a move in location was in order, we just weren't connecting and the tide was beginning to change.

The outgoing tide was starting to empty the bay exposing the occasional sandbar and the sloughs in between the bars. More and more real estate appeared as the tide made its way through the inlet and finally out into the ocean. Channels and cuts between the bars were becoming more pronounced. On the edge of a channel a small school of baitfish kept breaking water scattering and fleeing up onto the sand flats into just inches of water. This happened quite often and it became apparent that something was chasing them. Using an oar, so as not to spook the fish, we poled the boat over to the area quietly casting our jigs and spinner-rigs to the edge of the channel break and began a stop and go retrieve while maintaining contact with the bottom.

The object was to mimic an injured baitfish with our presentation.

Our first flounder came on the end of a long cast and more importantly on the spinner-rig while it was allowed to flutter downward. The second flounder was taken a lot closer to the boat, also on the spinner-rig as it fluttered downward. Several casts later yielded our third flounder even closer to the boat, but more importantly there were several flounder following the jig under the fish that was hooked on the spinner-rig and they were off the bottom in several feet of water trying to get the jig.

"The flounder clearly expressed an overwhelming interest in the jig as opposed to the spinner-rig even though both were baited with minnows."

Once again it was time to experiment with presentation only this time using jigs alone. Dragging and skittering the jig across the sandy bottom didn't work. Stop and go pauses didn't work. Hopping the jig across the bottom didn't work. However, each time the jig was retrieved up to the boat the flounder would follow along up to the surface (again expressing their interest in the bait and presentation) before darting back down into the depths of the murky water. Clearly something in the presentation was lacking.

Time to examine the facts

The jig was in the strike zone of the fish. They clearly expressed an interest in the jigs. They were hitting the spinner-rigs. Why were they hitting the spinner-rigs yet expressing more interest in the jigs?

The answer became obvious; a spinner-rig is lighter and sinks at a slower rate than the heavier jig. The slower rate of decent allows the spinner-rig to spend more time in the strike zone allowing the flounder ample time to catch the offering. Switching to a lighter (freshwater) jig was the key to our success and we caught many flounder that day using our newfound knowledge.

On each occasion valuable information was gained from the reactions of the flounder themselves including, the flounder is an ambush predator that relies on stealth and camouflage for survival. There is an acceptable strike zone which changes with water and weather conditions. We learned about the flounder's "natural instincts" to weed out the injured and weak. About the effectiveness of presentation with lures and baits to entice more strikes. And sometimes flounder do have a preferred food source.

DEEP-WATER FISHING

All of the basic principles outlined so far apply to deep-water fishing for flounder; natural instincts don't change with water depth. Flounder still utilize the drop-offs, flats, channels, points and funnels for feeding… only on a deeper level.

Here is where a chart of the area you plan to fish and the use of electronics come in handy. A good navigation chart will detail the various reefs, shoals, channels, flats, known shipwrecks and most importantly the "grid coordinates" of where they are located. It also shows water depth and contours. A global positioning system (GPS) will help get you there; a depth finder will help locate the structure and bottom details you are looking for, "you" still have to locate the fish. Once located, you can return to the exact position using the G.P.S. coordinates.

The same rule of multiple offerings applies when trying to locate flounder. Again you will need to experiment and adjust sinker-weight to hug the bottom according to the method of fishing you intend to do; especially if you intend to drift or troll. When fishing in water depths of 30 feet or more line diameter and water currents come into play. The more line you have out the more drag is created against the water which means more weight to stay down in the strike zone, otherwise your bait will start to plane. It will glide through the water like a kite on a string without much chance of making it to the strike zone. To compensate you must either reduce line diameter or increase the weight until you can actually "feel the bottom" through the fishing rod. This is where the thin diameter and strength of braided line comes into play. The result is less resistance, a better feel of what is going on down there, and the strength to land the big one.

Make sure the fishing rod is rated to handle the amount of weight you plan on using; otherwise you just may break the rod itself. If you plan on fishing deep water often consider medium-action saltwater gear to begin with as most deep water fishing is done vertically by jigging the rod straight up and down usually with heavy weights. This imparts "action" to the bait and helps to feel for any fish that may have subtly sucked in the bait. Also, if you do hook that fish of a lifetime, the rod will have the backbone to muscle it away from any structure and up to the boat quickly. A substantial amount of deep-water fishing is based around reef sites or wreck sites… lots of structure to get hung up on here.

Choosing Deep Water Baits

You want the bait to get noticed, investigated and eaten. Therefore, "the bigger the bait the better" rule applies when fishing deep. Big baits have more drag in the water and drift at a slower rate affording the flounder more of an opportunity to catch and eat the offering. Big baits rarely go unnoticed by big flounder because of their large appetites and the appeal of the bait. If fishing live bait use the largest bait in the bait well. When fishing cut baits "do not skimp on the fillet"; long, thin fillets are the most appealing to flounder… especially when used as a trailer on a jig. This presents your bait with a lot of bulk, scent and appeal, an offering that flounder find hard to resist.

When selecting spinner-rigs, choose a rig with the largest blades you can find. This will add a lot of thump and vibration that the flounder can feel and helps them target the location of the bait. Make the bait as easy to find and as appealing as you can for the fish.

You can also make your jigs easier to find and more appealing with the addition of rattles or spinner blades. Some jigs come with rattle chambers built in to the design or you can easily add them to enhance the effectiveness of any jig. The rattle chamber helps the fish locate the jig by sound. Shaking the fishing rod causes the shot in the rattle chamber to move back and forth emitting vibration and sound that the fish home in on. The addition of spinner blades to a jig adds flash, vibration and eye appeal for the fish. Freshwater anglers have been using these methods for years with much success; saltwater anglers can also benefit by using these tools. They are definitely worth adding to our flounder arsenal.

TARGETING BIG FLOUNDER

For flounder fishermen nothing gets the adrenalin pumping like hooking and landing a "big" flounder. I'm talking 6, 8, or 10-pound flounder.

"The kind of fish you have to fold over and stuff into the ice chest!"

These fish inhabit the oceans, bays, estuaries and inland waterways along our coastline from late spring through autumn. During the summer fishing season almost every fishing report will contain a segment about large flounder being caught by some lucky anglers. It is newsworthy and generates excitement amongst anglers and readers alike.

Now, it is possible to specifically target fish for big flounder, as they prefer larger than normal bait offerings. Cut baits such as sea robin, mackerel and squid in 4 – 6 inch lengths, large baitfish such as spearing, minnows and mullet, large jigs in the 1, 2 and 3 ounce sizes tipped with cut bait as a trailer are all attractive targets and easy meals for the big fish. These fish are attracted to slow moving bulky baits in and around their strike zone and will quite often pass up smaller forage waiting for a big meal to happen along. On the contrary, the smaller flounder often pass on the larger forage (no doubt intimidated by size and mass) opting for the smaller forage they are use to eating.

It adds up to: "Big bait equals big fish!"

However, there are occasions when even the big fish are being just as selective as its smaller counterparts. Only by experimenting with various baits (and sizes within these baits) will you be able to tell what their preference is at that given time. Sometimes they have a preference for small minnows and when they are on this bite you are going to catch a large percentage of smaller fish with the occasional big fish in between. They will exhibit a preference for the smaller minnows over the larger minnows of the same species. This becomes evident when the small minnows are catching fish and the large minnows go untouched while using the same basic setup on different fishing rods. Sometimes the small subtleties make a big difference between catching fish and just soaking your baits. This is particularly true when fishing shallow water flats and drop-offs.

Now backwater creeks and channels are a different story because here is where the big bait really shines. Creeks and channels are natural funnels governed by tidal movement. They contain submerged points, bends, drop-offs, flats and occasionally feeder streams with quick access to deep water, all of which are prime feeding stations and resting areas for fish in general but particularly so for the flounder. The baitfish swim around and relate to this natural structure and the predators follow, especially the bluefish. They feed with a reckless abandon showering the water column with bits and pieces of their victims as they chomp their way through the schools of baitfish. The remains are left to filter down along with other forage and are carried along in the current by the scouring action of the tides. Flounder and other bottom feeders lie in the natural funnel areas created by the channels waiting for an easy meal.

Prime Time for Fishing Channels

Although big flounder can be caught all throughout the summer months, late spring when the flounder first move into the bays, and late summer when the flounder move out of the bays, is the "prime time" to fish the primary (main) channels and inlets leading to and from the ocean.

Consider the primary channels as underwater highways or trails that fish use to enter and exit the bays. In the spring there is a constant influx of new fish arriving into the bays daily via these highways and trails. In late summer and early fall the flounder start to congregate around these channels and inlets once again as they migrate out of the bays and back into the ocean.

"During these seasons the primary channels are considered high percentage areas due to the concentration of fish moving into and through the area."

During the spring and early summer stick with the smaller jigs, baits and trailers as the forage base is generally small in size and not that active due to the water temperatures. Keep any cut baits and trailers 3 – 4 inches in length and around ¾ inch wide. This stout yet slender bait presents a very appealing profile for the flounder to eat and swallow with ease.

By midsummer the flounder are scattered throughout the bays, backwaters and estuaries. With the rise in water temperature the baitfish activity will increase along with boating activity as anglers seek out these prized fish. Flounder will follow the schools of baitfish into the backwater creeks and feeder streams along with the schools of bluefish and weakfish.

Midsummer Is the Prime Time to Fish Backwater Creeks

The backwater creeks and channels now contain a constant supply of food filtering throughout the system in a relatively concentrated area as compared to the wide expanse of the bay. The structure within these creeks (long sloping points, creek bends, feeder streams, etc.) helps to narrow the funneling effect and concentrate the flow of food and water even further, especially during periods of low tide.

Here is where a depth finder can help you determine the actual bottom contours and locate the narrowest portion of the creek channel. "These are high percentage areas" where fish will congregate to feed and rest in the deeper sections of the creek channel. Food is funneled through to the waiting fish with the tide changes and it does not take much of an effort for fish to secure a meal in these areas. It is during the periods of tidal movement that the majority of feeding occurs and now is when large bait (drifted through the funnel) will rarely go unnoticed because "large fish have large appetites."

Think large baits and jigs when fishing in these areas as the food filtering through the funnels is varied in size and mass. Here and now are when the flounder can afford to be selective about what and how often they eat. A large meal will satisfy a large hunger without the fish expending a lot of energy. That is the appeal large baits have on large flounder and why they work so well in these areas.

Fishing the Ebb Tide

Fishing during the ebb tide in backwater creeks can be just as productive as when fishing an incoming or outgoing tide change. Cast and retrieve (or troll) your offerings through and around the high percentage areas making sure you stay in contact with the bottom. The flounder are still there resting in the deep water of the channels waiting for the tide to change and the feeding cycle to begin again. Reach into your flounder arsenal and utilize the method to garnish the instinctive bite and let nature take over from there.

Another method to use is look for concentrations of baitfish such as minnows or spearing around jetties, bridge pilings, feeder creeks and sod banks. Grass flats hold a multitude of bait species such as shrimp, crabs, worms and baitfish and are generally a good area to fish. If you find the bait there's a good chance that you may find some fish in that area.

WHAT CAPTAINS HAVE TO SAY

Captain Howard Frank of the Salt Talk

With over twenty-years of experience here is what Captain Frank of the charter boat Salt Talk has to say on the subject:

"Flounder fishing is the bread and butter of my charter business during the summer months."

My clients book their charters with the expectations of catching fish. And as the captain, my job is to put my clients on fish. When the bite is slow or the fishing is tough this can put a lot of pressure on a captain to produce. While it is nice to have a high ratio of keepers to throw backs it is not always the case and not everyone understands this. However, this is fishing.

To locate flounder I look for drop-offs on channel edges where the bottom transition goes from fifteen to twenty-five feet in depth. The flounder will usually be lying somewhere along the drop-off or in the channel itself. Drift fishing in these areas will usually produce fish.

As far as baits and rigs go, I keep it simple and it works. Conventional rods spooled with 30lb. test line, a six-ounce weight and a plain hook on an eighteen-inch leader; baited with a strip of squid and/or minnow fished directly on the bottom. It is important to stay in contact with the bottom if you want to catch flounder with any consistency.

This combination is attractive to all size flounder as the big fish are mixed in with the smaller fish.

One on One with Captain Gary Seagraves

Early in the season look for flounder in the back-bay areas. These areas are the most fun and accessible areas to fish. With a small boat it's a blast, you can go almost anywhere and catch flounder. You don't need a lot of special gear or heavy weights to get to the fish either. The big females are in the back-bay areas until the water temperature reaches 68 degrees, and then they move out into deep water. When the bays are around this temperature you will catch lots of 16-inch flounder. Throughout the inlets and on the ocean side in front of the beaches, up to 2 miles out, you can catch lots of fish in the 17-inch range consistently. However, for really big fish you need to travel 5 miles out and fish around the deep-water wrecks in 150 to 200 feet of water. Here the big flounder are littered on the bottom all around the wreck sites.

"When you are after really big flounder search out the wrecks in deep water."

A friend of mine who is a wreck-diver came back one day and told me about all the giant flounder lying around the edges of the wreck. He later went back to fish the wreck and caught a 17-pound flounder in 190 feet of water. That's a very respectable fish.

I was fishing with some friends one day and the bites were slow, so being in the area I pulled up on the wreck and in 5 minutes we had two big fish in the boat. Because of the water depth 8-ounces of weight was needed to hold bottom using 30-pound tackle and big baits to entice the fish.

Now about the baits: "I use big baits. Bigger than most people would use and the flounder love it!"

I use bonito as bait. I fillet the sides and cut the fillets around 1 ¼ inch wide and from 4 to 6 inches in length leaving the skin on the strips. Flounder really eat these baits up. Another time I was fishing

53

for stripers and was using a whole 6-inch spot as bait when I felt something chomping on the bait. It kept chomping and chomping away. I knew it wasn't a striper because stripers like to run with the bait, so when the chomping stopped I set the hook and reeled up a 12-pound flounder. It had taken the whole spot in its mouth! "Big flounder eat big baits."

Captain Bill Kephart

Spring is the best time to catch big flounder in the back bays, as the big females are the first ones to migrate into the bays and spread out onto the flats because the shallow water warms quickly this time of year. Large cut baits such as mackerel or herring really grab their attention. Try to use fresh bait if possible and fish it close to the bottom. A freshly caught sea robin makes excellent cut bait; only instead of using the belly portion as most anglers do, fillet the entire side leaving the skin on. Cut the fillet into a wedge shape around 1½ -inches wide and about 4-inches long.

Later in the summer when the water temperature on the flats warms into the upper sixties and low seventies, look for the flounder to move back into the deeper channels where the water is cooler. If schools of large spearing move in with the warmer water that becomes my bait of choice. Flounder seem to gorge themselves on spearing when they are present and a 4-inch spearing spiraling along the bottom is an offering flounder find hard to resist. The large cut-baits also work extremely well in the depths of the channels where the flounder both feed and rest.

In the late summer look for the fish around the inlets and the main channels leading back into the ocean as they begin their migration to the wintering grounds offshore.

RONALD TRACY

Outdoor Writer, Photographer and Avid Flounder Fisherman

When it comes to flounder fishing, a little bit of knowledge goes a long way. It can mean the difference between catching fish and just spending a day on the water. And catching flounder is fun… exciting… and can be an easy thing to do! In all honesty, with a little bit of planning before hand a safe and enjoyable day can be had by everyone in your party. Here are a few tips worth remembering.

What season is it? In early spring the flounder are just beginning their migration into the bays via the inlets and channels leading to and from the ocean, making this a good starting point or a prime location. Secondary locations to try are the channels and flats in the surrounding area.

When summer arrives and the water temperature increases look for the fish to be scattered in the bay and backwater creek areas. Keep in mind that flounder are ambush predators with the ability to bury and blend into their surroundings. Drop-offs – the transitional area between shallow and deep water – are prime locations to find these fish. Secondary locations are the deeper water of the channels… especially in the backwater creeks during this time period.

In the late summer and into autumn, the fish will begin migrating back out into the ocean; once again via the channels and inlets. Again, these areas become the prime location to fish.

Fish your baits as close to the bottom as possible, hang onto your rod and you too, can become a successful flounder angler!

The Fishing Experience

To me, the fishing experience is more than just going out and catching a boatload of fish... a whole lot more. It is the culmination of many things from the camaraderie and enjoyment of time well spent with family and friends, the strengthening of bonds and relationships; memories that last a lifetime and refresh the body, soul and spirit. It fosters an awareness of the natural world around us and helps us to appreciate the beauty of nature; the outdoors, and all that our Creator has blessed us with.

It is a break in time from our often hectic lifestyles and offers us the chance to meet new people with mutual interests on common ground. We exchange knowledge with others so that everyone can enjoy in this wholesome and bountiful experience. And if we are lucky, somewhere along the way we will realize the need to conserve and protect this precious resource for future generations to come.

I was fortunate to have my longtime friend and saltwater mentor, Bill Kephart, take me under his wing and share his knowledge of saltwater fishing and conservation long before saltwater regulations came into effect. Now I try to share that knowledge with others whenever and wherever I can.

It is my hope that as you pass along your angling knowledge so that others may enjoy in our sport, you will also pass along what the fishing experience means to you along with the need for conservation and protection of this precious natural resource.

Summary

The information in these pages can help you to locate and catch more flounder in a variety of situations and water conditions. Remember also that daily bag and size limits, and flounder seasons, vary from state to state and sometimes year to year. Keep up with the current rules and regulations in the areas you intend to fish.

Congratulations! You now have the information needed to start catching flounder on a consistent basis. You know how to find likely areas that these fish utilize and why. We covered the baits that flounder find hard to resist and are proven winners. And let's not forget about the jigs and teasers… these are lures that flounder really love to eat. You have learned how to impart action to bait, make it stand out and attract attention. We covered the equipment you need for a successful outing.

I hope that you will consider this book as a primer for catching flounder. I spend a lot of time on the water chasing these fish and I am always learning something new. Believe me… there is no substitute for being out there on the water. You will learn from the fish. You will learn from other anglers. You can learn by watching other anglers who are catching the fish and remember… other anglers will be learning from you.

Do you know that the summer flounder can grow up to 3-inches a year?

It's true; the flounder you catch that is just under the size limit can return as a keeper next season, but only if you release it. Be selective when keeping a few fish for the table and return the rest to grow even larger for next season. You will be glad you did and you will be helping the resource at the same time. Thank you for reading Flounder Bytes and may all of your fishing trips be adventures!

GLOSSARY

Action – erratic movements imparted to bait or lures through the fishing rod to attract the attention of predatory game fish through sight, sound and sometimes vibration. Adding action to bait is used to entice strikes.

Backwater creek – smaller creeks and tributaries that feed into larger bodies of water such as bays, primary and secondary channels that eventually leads to the ocean.

Bait – a food substance or baitfish that is placed on a hook to attract and entice fish into eating through sight, smell and taste.

Baitfish – smaller fish used by anglers to attract and catch larger fish. State, Province or regional authorities generally regulate what fish species can be used as baitfish by anglers.

Barrel swivel – a device used to connect a leader, lure or weight to the main fishing line spooled on the reel. It is used to prevent line twist caused by the spinning motion of the bait or lure being used.

Bucktail jig – a name commonly associated with a lead-headed lure where the body is tied with hair or synthetic fibers around the shank of the hook.

Channel – the deepest part of a body of water where the current or flow of water passes through regularly.

Current – movement of water caused by tidal flow, wind action or a combination of the two.

Cut bait – usually a larger fish that is cut or filleted into strips or chunks that will fit and stay on the hook.

Drift fishing – utilizes wind and water current to move the boat around quietly while baited lines are lowered to the bottom and pulled behind the boat in search of fish.

Drop off – the transitional area between shallow and deep water; usually associated with channels or sand bars.

Feeder creek – small streams and creeks usually located in backwater areas that fill and empty during the change in tides. During the incoming tide - baitfish move into these areas to feed, during the outgoing tide - baitfish are pulled or swept out into the backwater creeks and channels.

Feeding station – an area where fish wait for food to come down via the current. The down current side of feeder creeks and funnel areas are prime feeding stations for fish due to the baitfish moving through these concentrated areas.

Flats – a long shallow area of relatively flat bottom generally six-feet or less in depth. Flats are often exposed during periods of low tides and are best fished on an incoming tide.

Flounder – a member of the flatfish family that has adapted to live on the seafloor. Highly regarded as a food and game fish species.

Flounder rig – In general, it consists of a hook (or hooks) tied to a length of fishing line with a weight attached by a drop line. It is attached to the end of your fishing line and is fished on the bottom.

Fluke – is another name for the summer flounder.

Funnel – a constricted area created by channel bends, sand bars and drop-offs. The food source (or baitfish) is concentrated as it flows through the constrictions and confines of these areas. Fish often set up feeding stations in and around these areas.

Grass shrimp – a small translucent crustacean found in and around various sea grasses and salt marshes. A prized bait for weakfish, flounder and various other species of fish.

High percentage area – an area or general location where fish are known to inhabit, feed or pass through during certain times of the fishing season. An example would be when flounder enter the bays during the early spring via the inlets and again during the fall migration back out to the ocean via the same inlets. During these time periods, the inlets are high percentage areas and this is a good place to concentrate your fishing efforts for the best results.

Hump – a raised area such as the top of a sand bar or the transitional area between two channels when submerged.

Inlet – the entrance to an inland bay or the mouth of a creek.

Instinctive strike – a natural reaction that predators have to the erratic or odd actions of their prey.

Jigs – an upturned hook with a weight molded or cast near the eyelet. The body may be dressed with hair, rubber or synthetic skirts.

Keeper – a fish that meets the minimum length or slot size requirements by law.

Lateral line – a nerve that grows down the sides of a fish - used to detect vibrations in the water. In appearance, it is a thin broken-black line. This line is located on the upper (or dark) side of the flounder.

Leader – a length of line that attaches the hook to the fishing line. Leader material is usually stronger, thicker and tougher than the line used to fill the spool on a fishing reel.

Length – the measurement from the tip of the head to the tip of the tail on a fish.

Limit – the amount of legal size keeper fish an angler may keep allowed by law. Limits and regulations vary by State and region.

Marker buoy – a floating device attached to a weighted line used to mark a specific location on and underneath the water.

Minnows – a small stout baitfish used by anglers to catch a wide variety of fish species.

Multiple offerings – the use of different types of baits or lures on separate fishing rods at the same time. Used to locate the fish and determine the most productive set-up.

Natural instinct – An innate reflex action enabling fish and wildlife to react without much thought.

Point – basically, a finger of land either above, below or extending down into the water.

Predator – carnivorous in nature; preys and depends upon other species for survival.

Presentation – the manner and actions an angler gives to the bait and how it is offered in order to entice a strike from the fish; for example: lethargic fish may require a slow presentation with little action imparted to the bait by the angler.

Primary locations – good starting point for locating fish, similar to a high percentage area with good fish holding features in or around the area.

Rigs – slang name for the different types of set-ups used on the business end of the fishing rod. Hooks, weights, jigs... etc.

Sand bar – an area of sand build up caused by strong tidal currents. Sand bars are often (but not always) exposed during

64

periods of low tide. The current flow of a storm surge may cause a sand bar to shift or erode.

Secondary locations - good backup locations to try if the primary location is not yielding fish.

Set up – the way a fishing rod is rigged including the baits, lures, weights and line being used to catch the fish.

Short – name for a fish that does not make the minimum size limit to be a keeper.

Sinker – cast or molded weight that is used to get the bait down to the fish.

Slot size – the minimum and maximum length a fish must be to be a legal keeper. Anything over or under the slot size must be released.

Sod bank – grass covered banks with sharp drops or undercut walls found scattered throughout inland waterways.

Spearing – a small slender baitfish translucent in color with a silver stripe running down each side of the fish. Also known as silversides.

Spinner-blade – metal blade attached to the line ahead of the fishhook, or attached to the wire portion of different types of lures. The blade revolves as it is pulled through the water.

Spinner-rig – a hook tied to a leader with spinner-blades attached. Used to attract and catch a variety of fish species.

Strike zone – the distance a fish is willing to travel to catch and eat bait.

Structure – submerged barriers either natural or manmade that fish and current must swim or flow around.

Tackle – the assorted equipment used to catch fish; rods, reels, lures, hooks and line, etc.

Teaser – a smaller lure, fly, bait or offering placed above the main bait on the fishing line. It is used to attract the fish's attention.

Tide – the periodic rise and fall of the ocean's water level on a daily basis. Both high and low tides occur twice daily.

Trailer – an added enticement placed on the hook of a jig to add bulk and appeal; for example, a strip of squid or a plastic worm.

Trolling – fishing in a boat where the speed and direction is controlled by the use of a motor, electric or gas powered, to cover an area thoroughly.

Water column – the different depths of a body of water.

Weight – a cast and molded sinker that attaches to the fishing line and gets the bait down to the fish.

30118638R00043

Made in the USA
San Bernardino, CA
05 February 2016